Oil, Share, Repeat

A BLUEPRINT TO LAUNCHING YOUR BUSINESS IN 3 DAYS

DORY DOYLE

PRINTED BY: DOYLE ADVENTURES, LLC

Thank You

First of all, thank you to my husband, Tim. Without you these last 15 years, I don't know where I would be. Thank you for encouraging me when I was too scared or defeated to get out of bed, and thank you for being my front-row fan during my greatest accomplishments. Most of all, thank you for being my partner in this business and in life.

Thank you to Niccole, for your guidance and mentorship in this business. You have been the voice in my head and in front of me during my biggest decisions, and it has been an honor to tackle and conquer this endeavor together. Our friendship shows how this business can enrich our lives in a way that isn't found on a paycheck.

Thank you to my OBAAT team. Without you, I never would have realized the need for the simple explanation, and I wouldn't have had the practice at explaining it. Especially thanks to Beth, Rachel, Tina, Kristen, and Stephanie and my crossline friends Melissa, Melissa, Dorie, and Danielle for your advice, feedback, and early excitement over this project.

Finally, thank you to my parents, Elly and Tucker, who showed me both the value of work ethic and also working ethically. To this day, you continue to show me what love, respect, and commitment can bring to our lives.

This book is dedicated to my Papa Alan, who inspired me to do what makes me happy and to follow my entrepreneurial spirit.

ABOUT DORY

I joined Young Living in August 2014, after 3 months of researching and asking questions about oils to my enroller and sponsor. I wanted to understand why Young Living was marketed as a network marketing model and why I needed to get the full kit. And throughout that research phase, I continued to resist the business side of it. Well, once my oils were in my hands, I saw how they worked for my family, including my 10 month old twins. It was then that I realized that I had inevitably been sharing and teaching about essential oils, just by talking about my experiences to my friends. I decided to borrow a script and teach my first class. Within a month, one class turned into four. By November, I was a Senior Star, and by May 2015, I was an Executive.

I achieved Silver just 5 months after first becoming an Executive, and although I maintained for 3 months, I fell into a common trap and burned out. In January 2016, I was thrilled to have earned Silver Retreat, but I lost my drive and consistency and took the month off. One month turned into more.

2016 was a difficult year in my business. Once I lost my momentum, it was hard to build up that consistency again. I suffered a series of setbacks, and I would have been justified in walking away. For a moment, I nearly caved to those challenges and self-pity, but I didn't. We all have excuses and setbacks, but it was my decision and conscious effort to move forward.

Those experiences taught me to lean on my upline and crossline friends. I came to understand how powerful this business could be, not just because of the paycheck, but also because of the relationships that came from the experience. Young Living wasn't just a product and a way to structure a business, but it brought together people who all had an idea (wellness) at different levels, and we could work with and learn from each other.

Towards the end of 2016, as I regained my Silver rank and began working towards Gold and beyond, I realized that focusing on the people in my organization was the key. I began listening, asking questions, comprehending, coaching, and instilling confidence. And without that and my experiences with my amazing One Breath at a Thyme community, this book couldn't have been possible. My name is on the cover, but this whole book is based on the coaching, questions, workshops, and trainings that I have done with and because of my team.

I am a real person. I am doing all of this with a husband, twin preschoolers, a dog, and a home. I am involved in my children's schools, and our family actively participates in therapies, education planning meetings, after-school activities, and our synagogue. Young Living is my full-time job, but it is possible to have the other roles in your life and find abundance as well.

The Overview

The whole purpose of this book is to help you build a business with Young Living. It is easy to over-complicate the process, but that's not necessary. Use this book as your guide: pick it up, read it, follow each of the steps, and if you continue to do the work, you will have a Young Living business. Does this mean that you won't have ups and downs? High and low seasons? Oh, you'll have that. But with consistency, you will build a business that you will be proud of and that others will respect.

When you are ready to start in the Young Living business, you may want to learn everything. As leaders, we won't tell you everything... because even after years of doing this, we are still learning. This is a company where you learn as you go, and every year or two it changes on you. It's pretty amazing, actually!

So I have broken it down into an easy-to-follow path of what you need to know when you're ready to know it. This book is meant to get your business up and running.

But I want to be sure that you understand: this is a business. If you treat it with professionalism, respect, and hard work, you will experience growth and the benefits from that work ethic. Likewise, if you wish to see growth in your business, then commit to consistently doing the work.

At the same time, this is a business of relationships. You cannot expect to grow your Young Living business without others. So while you are treating your business with respect, don't forget that the way that you treat others will also determine your success.

How?

You want to do this as a business, but you don't know how to get started. You may be overwhelmed or you just don't know what to do first.

It's ok! Stop. Pull out the closest oil to you. Breathe it in deeply and let out the biggest audible sigh possible. Seriously, this book will still be here.

My Calming Oils

Now, stop overthinking. The name of this book gives you your blueprint. You will build your business by doing these three things:

Oil,
Share,
Repeat

Oil

This is your hub. Your foundation for everything in your business. I want you to fall in love with these products. Be a product of the product. Love Young Living and the healthy lifestyle that you can achieve with our products. I encourage you to take advantage of the monthly promotions so you can maximize your rewards each month and get as many free items as possible.

Share

You will find that that is the majority of this book. I have actionables listed at each step and will lay out the blueprint for making your business happen. **This is where the 3 E's come in:**

1. EDUCATE

2. ENROLL

3. EMPOWER

Repeat

The goal for you is to have systems in place that work at the Distributor level but will take you right on up through Diamond. And yes, I will give you the tools to make it happen. Keep reading!

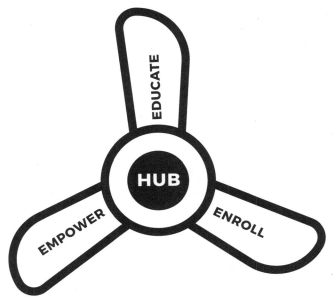

Your Why

The first question you should ask yourself when you want to start a new (ad)venture... why?

- **Why is this interesting to me?**
- **Why will this help me?**
- **Why is this important to me?**
- **Why do I want to do this?**
- **Why do I desire something different?**

This *Why* is more important than any *How* or *What* or *Who*. Because without a passion for what you are doing, every little road bump is going to feel like a mountain.

Before you start dreaming and set some goals, I first want to share the possibilities with you. This is our Income Disclosure Statement. These are real dollar amounts made by real people. While the exact amount depends on your enrollments and downline's continued purchases, these numbers are absolutely possible.

Ask your enroller why they have shared Young Living with you and others. Your enroller's Why:

YOUNG LIVING 2016 U.S. INCOME DISCLOSURE STATEMENT

As a direct selling company selling essential oils, supplements, and other lifestyle products, Young Living offers opportunities for our members to build a business or simply receive discounts on our products.

Whatever your interest in the company, we hope to count you among the more than 2 million Young Living members joining us in our mission to bring Young Living essential oils to every home in the world.

What are my earning opportunities?

Members can earn commissions and bonuses as outlined in our Compensation Plan. As members move up in the ranks of Young Living, they become eligible for additional earning opportunities.

This document provides statistical, fiscal data about the average member income and information about achieving various ranks.

RANK	PERCENTAGE OF ALL MEMBERS[3]	MONTHLY INCOME[4]				ANNUALIZE AVERAGE INCOME[5]	MONTHS TO ACHIEVE THIS RANK[6]		
		Lowest	Highest	Median	Average		Low	Average	High
Distributor	94.0%	$0	$841	$0	$1	$12	N/A	N/A	N/A
Star	3.5%	$0	$811	$60	$77	$924	1	15	255
Senior Star	1.3%	$1	$5,157	$197	$240	$2,880	1	22	255
Executive	0.6%	$50	$12,139	$434	$514	$6,168	1	29	253
Silver	0.2%	$562	$25,546	$1,783	$2,227	$26,724	1	36	251
Gold	0.1%	$1,781	$46,820	$4,874	$6,067	$72,804	1	54	240
Platinum	< 0.1%	$5,146	$85,993	$12,188	$15,324	$183,888	2	63	238
Diamond	< 0.1%	$14,898	$140,333	$32,078	$39,566	$474,792	10	75	251
Crown Diamond	< 0.1%	$37,227	$232,551	$64,256	$74,188	$890,256	14	83	236
Royal Crown Diamond	< 0.1%	$58,392	$262,864	$155,248	$152,377	$1,828,524	17	106	230

The income statistics in this statement are for incomes earned by all active U.S. members in 2016. An "active" member is a member who made at least one product purchase in products in the previous 12 months. The average annual income for all members in this time was $25, and the median annual income for all members was $0. 51% of all members who enrolled in 2015 did not make a purchase with Young Living in 2016. 57% of all members who enrolled in 2014 did not continue with Young Living in 2016.

Note that the compensation paid to members summarized in this disclosure do not include expenses incurred by a member in the operation or promotion of his or her business, which can vary widely and might include advertising or promotional expenses, product samples, training, travel, telephone and Internet costs, and miscellaneous expenses. The earnings of the members in this chart are not necessarily representative of the income, if any, that a Young Living member can or will earn through the Young Living Compensation Plan. These figures should not be considered as guarantees or projections of your actual earnings or profits. Your success will depend on individual diligence, work, effort, sales skill, and market conditions. Young Living does not guarantee any income or rank success.

[1] Based on a count of all active members in 2016.
[2] Because a distributor's rank may change from during the year, these percentages are not based on individual distributor ranks during the year, but based on the average distribution of distributor ranks during the entire year.
[3] Because a distributor's rank may change from during the year, these incomes are not based on individual distributor incomes throughout the entire year, but based on earnings of all distributors qualifying for each rank during any month throughout the year.
[4] This is calculated by multiplying the average monthly incomes by 12.
[5] These statistics include all historical ranking data for each rank and thus is not limited to people who achieved these ranks in 2016.
[6] These incomes include income earned from January 1, 2016, and December 31, 2016, but which was paid between February 2016 and January 2017.
[7] Members who do not make at least one product purchase in the previous 12 months have their membership terminated.

YOUNG LIVING
ESSENTIAL OILS

Envision

Do it. Start now. What is your Why?
Draw, glue, write, dream below:

Need some help jogging your memory? These prompts may help you!

What are you experiencing now?
(on a scale from 1-10, 1 = false 10 = true)

I am not stressed about finances

I am debt free

I have plenty of money in savings

I feel financially prepared for the future

I am having the experiences I want (travel, education/self improvement, lifestyle, etc.)

I am living my dreams

I feel inspired & fulfilled doing what I do

I spend as much time as I want with those I care about

I am making a difference (service, charitable giving, etc.)

Things that make me, Me:

My path leads to:

Potential road bumps:

Creative opportunities:

Daily activities to get me there:

1 month goal:

6 month goal:

1 year goal:

I, _____, commit to my Young Living business for the next 4 years*, until _____.

Signed:

_____

*Why 4 years? After you consistently work the business for 4 years, you will see that you have gained traction, excitement, and potentially life-changing income.

Be Coachable

> Coachable: capable of being easily taught and trained to do something better

I hope that you will find this book to be exactly what you need to launch your Young Living business. But if you learn nothing else, please learn this: be coachable.

For as long as you are green, you can grow.
—Mother Teresa

There are so many reasons why you should be coachable in any business:

- There are others who have had the same experience as us.
- It forms connections with others.
- It allows us a chance to grow professionally.
- We don't have all the answers.
- If we aren't working on personal development, then nothing in our business will flourish.

Experience teaches only the teachable.
—Aldous Huxley

Without being coachable, we will not grow. I'll tell you a story: when I went to Silver Retreat in 2016, I was not currently at the rank of Silver. I had been "stuck" at Executive for the past 9 months. I had only attained the rank of Silver for 3 months in 2015. Yes, I did earn the trip and my Silver rank, but I longed to be back at Silver and working steadily towards Gold and beyond.

So I took the opportunity to learn. I soaked it all in. My husband and I were lucky enough to spend almost the entire retreat with my Diamond leader Niccole Perez and her husband. It was an intense trip, but one that allowed me to really reflect in what had been happening to my business over the last year. Although I didn't necessarily agree with each idea that we talked about, I listened. And I asked questions. When I got home, I implemented.

I ranked back up to Silver the very next month, and I never looked back. A year later after I truly regained Silver, I became a steady (and growing) Gold.

From that experience, I learned to take every opportunity to learn from those around me. At the events that I attend, I make sure to talk to as many people as I can. And not just talking and saying "hi," but actually talking and learning from them. Actively listening. I reach out to leaders via social media as well. And not just leaders who are ranked with me or higher than me. A leader is defined by how you carry yourself, not your title. There are many of my team members who have taught me valuable lessons.

Be willing to be a beginner every single morning.
—Meister Eckhart

Take this book and learn from it. Follow it. And then take the basic skills and strategies you learned here and grow from learning from others. You will connect with some leaders and not others. That's ok. Give yourself and others that grace.

But for you, listen with an open mind. Leave your inhibitions at the door. You are about to start a wonderful journey with so much promise.

List 3 things that you love about yourself.

List 2 things that you wish to learn.

List 1 person that you can go to RIGHT NOW as a mentor.

Personal Development

Ask any leader in Young Living, and we will all tell you that personal development is one of the biggest factors of success in this business. Personal development is the reflection piece of being coachable.

Along with your health, you must take an introspective look at yourself. You cannot expect to be an effective leader if you do not grow. There are various ways that I suggest starting on your personal development path:

Color Personality Test

There are many personality tests on the market, but one of my favorites is in Jacob Adamo's book, *Full Spectrum Success*, and also on his website: jacobadamo.com. This outlines the 4 color personalities, but you can also find that you might be a bit of a rainbow! What I love most about this simple but effective book is that I have learned that my colors have different shades: troublesome, typical, and true. As you settle in to your true self, you find so much more balance and understanding of our colors and how you can effectively communicate with those around us.

Aroma Freedom Technique (AFT)

AFT is a step-by-step process created by Dr. Benjamin Perkus and is designed to be learned and used by anyone who wants more freedom in their life. It is an entirely new approach to aromatherapy, one that uses the power of pure essential oils to instantly and irresistibly shift a person's mental state, mood, and ability to take positive action. Through this process you will learn how to identify what you really want in life, what is blocking you, and how to release these blocks in a matter of minutes. Then, you learn a daily practice to keep you on track. You can find more information and connect with an AFT Practitioner (like myself) at aroma-freedom. myshopify.com/. The beauty of AFT, however, is that you can learn to walk yourself through a session!

Books

There are a lot of good books for personal and professional growth. You can find in-depth list in the companion to this book: *Propel*, by Niccole Perez.

I will talk more on personal development as it relates to positivity and positive self-talk on page 42.

Take the color personality test at Jacob Adamo's website. Write down your results:

_____ % Red _____ % Blue _____ % Green _____ % Yellow

Talk to your enroller about the next 3 books you should read.

My Health Focus

Before you can help others, you must have a love of these products yourself. Notice, I didn't say that you have to be a picture-perfect poster child for health, wellness, and beauty. In fact, a work in progress is perfect—you are relatable and approachable. Using the space provided, get together with your enroller and map out your health and wellness goals and your current plan.

HEALTH GOALS

Research and Resources

Name:
Starting Date:
Goal Date:

Month 1	Month 2	Month 3	Month 4	Month 5	Month 6
Health Goals	Health Goals	Health Goals	Health Goals	Health Goals	Health Goals
Products	Products	Products	Products	Products	Products
Lifestyle Changes	Lifestyle Changes	Lifestyle Changes	Lifestyle Changes	Lifestyle Changes	Lifestyle Changes

Share

We all have strengths. Some of us have a social media presence. Some get along great with people individually. Some have never met a stranger. And some can command a room when they walk in. As you start your Young Living business, don't change how you communicate with others. This is not the time to start a public Facebook page or experiment with a different social media platform. Use the strengths you already have, while being open to fine-tuning.

Social Media

"Facts tell, stories sell." There is a lot of truth to that. By telling your story and your experience (how you feel when you use the product), you are going to help others to understand how they will feel when they use your products. There is so much to say about social media, and with as fast as it is changing, I want you to go to experts. There have been countless books, articles, and videos on the subject, so I encourage you to search that out. That being said, don't start something just because you think that it will sell oils. Do something that is true to you.

1 on 1s

It might be slower starting, but by meeting people one-on-one, you are going to accomplish a lot of things.

1. You are forming a relationship—a friendship—with that person. Friendships lead to trust. And with trust, there's a lot that you can accomplish in this business.

2. You can ask the right questions. Find out why that person is interested in a healthier lifestyle and our product lineup. What do they want to accomplish? This allows you to tailor your conversation to their needs.

3. You can enroll that member easier. Instead of asking a general question of "who is ready to get started?" you can read body language, ask questions, and address hesitancies privately. It's a personal connection, one that will help take your business and that member much further.

Workshops and Events

Workshops and events are great options for those that want to talk to a lot of people at once. There are definitely some strategies that you want to implement in order to have a successful experience. I have a whole section on workshops later in the book. For even further information, check out Niccole Perez's book, *Propel*.

Cold Market

A warm market is made up of the people that you already know (or people your friends know). A cold market is everyone else. But it only takes 1 conversation to turn a cold market into a warm one.

Unless you have experience at this, cold marketing may not be successful for you initially. It doesn't mean that you shouldn't attempt it (because we have had some wonderful new members come from cold marketing), but I want you to be careful of falling into the common pitfalls:

1. Posting about sales and products. Frankly, no one really cares. Without the personal connection to you, it may feel like crickets. And with social media algorithms as they are, if you don't know what you're doing, no one will see them.

2. Starting separate business pages to promote your product. To do this successfully, you need to have an audience base. Your best bet is to utilize your personal social media platforms and combine your personal + YL posts to showcase the YL Lifestyle.

Focus on your favorite oil or product. How do you feel when you use it (happy, relaxed, grounded, energized, alert, etc)? Use that description and share it with one person today.

FORM Relationships

FORM stands for Family, Occupation, Recreation, and Motivation/ Message. Simply put, these are the types of questions and methods of framing conversations so that you can learn more about the other person. In a conversation with someone else, you will want to ask more questions and allow the other to talk more than you.

FAMILY*

- Where are you from?
- What brought you to the area?
- How long have you lived _____?
- Tell me about your family.
- What is is like being the _____ in/of _____?
- How did you meet your partner?
- Have you heard from (*mutual friend*) recently?

OCCUPATION

- What is it that you do?
- What do you love about your job? Is it rewarding?
- I'd love to hear more about your business.
- Did you go to school for that?
- How long have you been with _____?
- What made you go into that line of work?

RECREATION

- I love your _____. Where did you get them?
- I also enjoy _____. How did you get started in it?
- Do you have any suggestions for a restaurant I can try?
- What do you do when you're not working?
- Do you follow sports?
- What was the last movie you saw?
- What did you think of it?

MOTIVATION/MESSAGE

- What in the past has made you the happiest?
- What did you dream of doing when you were a child?
- Aside from your work and hobbies, what is important to you?
- What is your goal right now?
- What are some things on your bucket list?

*Avoid asking how many children someone has or if they will have any more. This will make sure that if there is a history of infertility or child loss, you can be sensitive of this.

I want to explain why FORMing is so important. No one cares about what you have to say until they felt heard. It's a hard truth, but look at your social interactions, and you'll see how true it is. When you've met someone for the first time, what made you feel heard? Probably being able to talk and tell your story.

So when you have a conversation with someone else and they ask you a question ("How old are your kids?"), you can follow up your answer with a question back to them ("I have a 3 and 5 year old. How old are yours?"), asking the same thing.

This is a business where we do have a catalog and products for sale. Though you are not actually taking orders, you are still selling a product based on your excitement and connection with that person's needs. You may get caught up in telling everyone everything that you know. But that is much less important than the connection that you have with others. So instead of verbal explosions, learn about someone's love of reading, but they just feel so stressed that they can't do it anymore. That's when you can suggest setting up a diffuser with some calming oils in their reading nook. Or the mom who is so frazzled that she forgets to drink water. Suggest your favorite ingestible oil that now can be stored next to her glass water bottle. Now, these products actually mean something to them.

The Color Personalities & FORMing

Now that you know a little bit about the color personalities, you may start recognizing different personalities in different people. In a conversation with someone else, for instance, you may ask the following:

RED What are your priorities?	**YELLOW** Who would find meaning in this?
GREEN How important is this to you?	**BLUE** Why is this important to you?

The way that you connect with a person and speak their language will help both of you to feel more comfortable in that conversation.

Run a Workshop

Leading an event doesn't have to be intimidating. Follow these twelve steps to manage and run a successful workshop.

1. Know who is **hosting** the event, whether it is you or someone else. If someone else, have a hostess gift for them (flowers, a special sample bottle of product, or something else that would be meaningful to them).

2. Create a **guest list.**

3. **Write a description** that explains how this event will fill a need (health topic, fun, night out, pampering, hot topic, etc) to create a desire in others to attend. This can be used for Facebook webinars, workshops, groups, events, or for face-to-face marketing.

4. **Invite*** those on your guest list at least 2 weeks before the event. Ask other members of your organization to show up at your workshop. This validates and edifies you as an educator and brings in the fellowship piece of what you do.

5. **Follow through** individually with your guests. Understand that some people will not respond. Some may plan on attending, but cancel. Typically 10-20% of your invited list will actually attend the event, but it takes personal follow-up instead of just passive posts.

6. Create and practice your **script/outline** for your event. There are many options out there, and *Propel* gives you a great option for writing your own script. It's better to cover less information (it is more effective and less overwhelming).

7. **Follow through** with guests in the 1-2 days leading up to the event. This should be a combination of posts (if utilizing a social media event platform) and individual messages. Teasers and some basic information is great to pique interest.

8. Show up to your workshop 30-60 minutes early with **minimal set up**.

9. **FORM** your guests as they enter. Ask them to write their information on your sign-in sheet.

10. **Teach**, limiting your talk to 30-45 minutes. Make sure to have interactive portions (even standing up) so guests stay alert. Use your script and the Wellness Workshop Notes. Also, have someone introduce you to edify you so that others will listen to what you have to say.

11. End with a **strong close**. Let them know how they can buy. Limit questions and instead allow them to ask you one-on-one. Why? Listening to someone else's question might be the difference between that decision to buy and waiting. If they walk out of the room, they probably will not purchase.

12. **Follow through** with each guest consistently. Send thank you notes for attending, call, or text.

*Need suggestions? Ask your upline leader!

A Note on Edification:

Edification is when you offer positive information about another person or a company. It is one of the most important skills that you can learn in network marketing—and really in your life! It is important to edify upline, downline, and crossline. Here's why:

- Builds confidence, authority and trust for the audience and presenter
- Gives prospects an inside look into a strong team culture
- Tells the prospect why they should listen to the presenter
- Sets the tone for the entire presentation
- Even if you don't feel confident in yourself yet, you can be confident in your leader

Put your next workshop on your calendar, at least 2 weeks from now. Focus on doing all of the steps!

How Can You End a Conversation?

I want to give you permission to do something that might be a little outside your comfort zone. It is ok to end your conversations (and your workshops and events) with a strong close. You do not have to feel guilty to tell someone how to get started with Young Living or ask for their information to connect with them again. Remember, your business will not move forward unless you have new people join. For more information on strong closings for your events, please read Niccole Perez's book, *Propel.*

While in the checkout line at the store, meeting a friend, or talking to a co-worker, use some of the FORMing prompts to learn more about them. Ask more questions!

Sign Up Members

Ok, now we're getting into logistics. But it can still be incredibly easy and replicable. After all, if you can do this in a simple way, your team members can do this with simplicity too.

1. Use a YL Link Builder to give your personal sign-up link (one is available in the Virtual Office under Member Resources).

2. Walk them through the sign up if needed. Make sure to talk to them about Essential Rewards:

- A monthly wellness box program

- You can customize your box each month with price points

- Earn free products AND points towards products of your choosing (10-25% back)

- Flexibility

- This is the plan for those who want to make serious lifestyle improvements in home cleaning, personal care, family health, pet needs, makeup, and replenishing your used supplies.

3. Send them a welcome packet and reference material. Talk to your enroller to get suggestions for gifts. Make sure to refer to Policy & Procedures to learn limits and guidelines.

4. Add them to your upline's membership or oil education group.

5. Further support them and check in as needed.

Time to prepare for your next enrollment! Pull your YL Link and save it so you can easily share it the next time you talk to someone about Young Living.

Essential Rewards

Establish a Lifestyle

The most crucial time of a member's time with Young Living are the first 3 months. If they feel supported and excited, they will trust you to join Essential Rewards. And if they are on ER for 4 months, we have found that they will be on it for the long term.

You have goals. Your members have goals. And you can help achieve those goals through complementary products from the Young Living catalog.

Essential Rewards is not just an autoship program, it is a healthy lifestyle.

Loyalty Rewards

Members have the ability to earn rewards for being on the Essential Rewards, when consecutive orders are placed at 3, 6, 9 and 12 months. Plus, you'll get an exclusive blend at the 12 month mark.

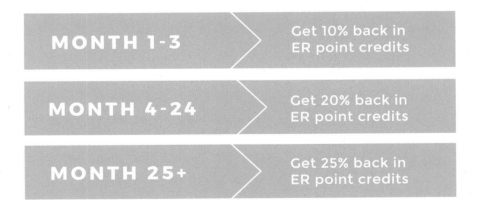

MONTH 1-3 — Get 10% back in ER point credits

MONTH 4-24 — Get 20% back in ER point credits

MONTH 25+ — Get 25% back in ER point credits

You can use the Health Goals Worksheet from page 19 to create a strong groundwork for wellness and freedom. You can print out more copies of this at our website www.inspiredsharing.com.

Ask a friend if you can sit down to help them fill out a Health Goals Worksheet. Bonus points if they aren't a member yet!

Teach: Top 3

When you get started with your Young Living business, the last thing I want is for you to be a walking encyclopedia. No one can replicate that. The more you try to know, the less people will copy you and follow in your footsteps. By limiting yourself to top 3 suggestions, then you will have a much easier-to-replicate business model. And it's less overwhelming. After all, can you imagine if someone just presented you with a full catalog with 600+ items and you had to pick what you wanted?

What is your niche right now? Which of these categories interests you? Pick one and fill in your top 3 products. This will give you the insight in which products you should learn about (and teach to others).

Top 3 Oils

Top 3 Supplements

Top 3 Vitamins

Top 3 Home Cleaning

Top 3 Personal Care

Top 3 Kids Products

Teach: Consumables

After my first Convention experience, I realized that if I only focus on our essential oils, I am constantly searching for new members. That's because a member will purchase a PSK with oils and diffuser, use them here and there, and although they may need to reorder, those oils last a long time. So in order to keep building your business, you need to keep finding new members.

If, however, I am teaching our members and prospectives about the consumables from our product lineup, I will develop members for life.

What is a consumable?

Anything that is used on a consistent basis and will be replaced in 1-4 months.

Most-Often Used Consumables:

- **Supplements**
- **Vitamins**
- **Hand soap**
- **Toothpaste**

Other Consumables:

- **Baby line**
- **Cleaning line**
- **Shampoo/Conditioner**
- **Lotion**
- **Mineral makeup**
- **Men's line**

Non-Consumables

- **Oils***
- **Skincare***

*While considered "consumables" because they are used up and need to be reordered, it takes longer to go through these products.

Create a sample 3-month order (100 PV) using only consumables. This is something you can present to your members!

Teach: Transfer Buying

Transfer Buying is when you replace the products you would have purchased at the store with products from the Young Living catalog.

This promotes the benefits of Essential Rewards, because you aren't spending MORE each month. You are spending DIFFERENTLY each month. You are transferring your spending from the grocery store to your YL order.

And then on top of that, teach about the points you get back, the loyalty gifts, the reduced shipping, and the extra promos. It's a no-brainer!

STEP 1: Go through each room of your home. On the Transfer Buying Worksheet, highlight the products you have in your home.

STEP 2: Look at your options from the YL catalog and write down what products you will try.

STEP 3: Select at least $100/100 PV from the list. These products become your 100 PV Essential Rewards order. Remember, if you go above that, you will earn more free products and points!

Plan out your next 2 months of orders, using the Transfer Buying form. By doing it yourself, you will know how to help your members do the same.

Bathroom

Shampoo/Conditioner:
Bath/Body Bar Soaps:
Body Wash:
Bath Bombs/Salts:
Body Oil:
Body Lotion:
Ointment:
Sports Cream:
Shaving Cream:
Aftershave:
Face Wash:
Face Scrub:
Face Toner:
Face Serum:
Face Moisturizer:
Eye Cream:
Wrinkle Cream:
Toothpaste:
Dental Floss:
Mouthwash:
Hand Soap:
Deodorant:
Makeup:
Perfume:
Cologne:
Kids Body Wash:
Kids Lotion:
Kids Shampoo:
Kids Toothpaste:
Kids Diapering Needs:
Toilet Bowl Cleaner:
Shower Spray:
Bathtub Scrub:

Cleaning Cabinet

Carpet Freshener:
Glass Cleaner:
Stainless Steel Cleaner:
Tile Cleaner:
Laminate and Hardwood Floor Cleaner:

Laundry Room

Laundry Soap:
Fabric Softener:
Stain Remover:
Dryer Sheets:

Kitchen

Dish Soap:
Dishwasher Detergent:
Hand Soap:
Fruit and Veggie Wash:
Degreaser:
Oven Cleaner:
Bleach:
Goo Remover:

Animal Products

Deodorizer:
Dental Chews:
Shampoo/Wash:
Ointment:

Car/Purse/Misc.

Cleaning Wipes:
Air Freshener/Wall Plugs:
Candles:
Fabric Spray:
Linen Spray:

Vitamin/Supplement Cabinet

Throat Lozenges:
Multivitamin:
Enzymes:
Mineral:
Calcium:
Vitamin B:
Vitamin C:
Antioxidants:
Probiotics:
Essential Fatty Acids:
Protein Shake:
Insect Repellant:
Sunscreen:

Holiday + Gift Ideas:

Wedding:
Housewarming:
New Baby:
Anniversary:
Birthday:
Christmas:
Mother's Day:
Father's Day:
Teacher:
Graduation:

Make a Change Challenge

For many of you, this may have been the entire reason for you to purchase this book. I have been leading the Make a Change Challenge for a couple of years with my team, and it has been highly effective. It is now one of the only incentives that we do in our online community.

How it Works:

- Members on ER agree to purchase one new-to-them product every month (making a change with their current products)
- Products must be consumables (non oils)
- Members try the product and post a review in our education group
- At the end of 3 months, the members will receive a product credit

Why It Works:

- Must be on ER (raising ER rates)
- Try out new products
- Learn how to write about the products
- Take interesting pictures and post to social media
- Gain experience talking intelligently about a product (easier when they want to share with others)
- Content on your team's education page
- Get ideas from other members on what to order next
- Intrinsically motivate (they don't know the product credit amount. They don't have to spend a certain amount of money. They just get to participate and contribute)

There it is. It's simple, effective, and easy to run. Members are self-motivated, and you can gain a lot of positive momentum from this challenge I have gone from 22% of my members on Essential Rewards in 2016 to 42% because of the benefits from this challenge.

Don't have an oil usage group? You can still start a Make a Change Challenge with your members. Have them post to their personal page or social media accounts and tag you or use a fun hashtag. This way your whole team sees the posts!

The Earning Opportunity

Per the most recent Income Disclosure Statement, most of Young Living members are just that: members. This is wonderful, because it means that a vast majority of our product users (millions of people) are so in love with our products that they continue to purchase them without earning any income.

But for those who are interested in taking it further, there is a lot of opportunity for growth and financial freedom. As a way to further empower your members, it is worth your time to educate them on the income opportunity with their Young Living membership.

I've learned the hard way—at least let them know that the business opportunity exists. It's not a requirement, but it provides a very real way of earning income or at least paying for your products.

What do you say? Here's an idea:

"Hi _____! I am so thrilled that you have been loving your Young Living products like I have. They have made quite the difference in both of us, haven't they? I've never slept better! I wanted to let you know that in the last _____ (weeks/months/years) I've been using and loving Young Living, and I have decided to share the products with others so they can feel as good as I do. I love how you inspire others through your posts about _____. If I sent you a copy of *Oil Share Repeat*, would you spend 20 minutes a day for the next 3 days reading it? Then we can talk about it when you're done."

> **3-2-1: Make a list of 3 people that would benefit from the Young Living business, 2 people that you think have great personalities for it, and 1 person that you are going to talk to today.**

Using Your Resources

As a way to further educate your members, utilize the Health Goals Worksheet and Transfer Buying Form both in this book and via our website www.inspiredsharing.com. Use them to help coach your members and grow your business!

But it doesn't stop there. Tap into your upline leaders' groups for further education and classes for yourself and your members. Reach out to your closest leaders and ask for them to mentor you in goal setting and implementation. You might even be able to find accountability partners to pair with on this journey.

Just remember that you are not alone in this. You have a team of people that can help you to feel empowered and to support your members. You don't have to be everything to everyone. Use your resources.

Personally invite your members to your Silver+ leader's next workshop. This allows you to build further relationships and edify your leaders. When your members attend more workshops taught by more people, it further supports the good things that you're teaching them.

Repeating the Steps

Now we get to Repeat! In the pages that follow, you will learn the systems to repeat over and over again to grow your business.

Your goal is to have self-sustaining legs. This means that others do what you are doing. It doesn't mean that they are you, because you are unique. You bring gifts and talents to the table that others may not be able to copy. Nobody can be you (and they shouldn't try to be), but they can take your system (or the systems outlined in this book) and make it work for them.

This is duplication of steps and systems.

It's utilizing something like this book—something that anyone can pick up, follow as a guide, and then run with the business. It's having a set way of doing things that can be copied easily.

Can you still add your own pizzaz and pop to make your business unique? Yes. Absolutely. But don't feel like you need to or should reinvent the wheel. Stick to the things that make the business grow:

- Focus on the Hub: using oils and personal development
- Sharing with education, enrollments, and empowering others
- Repeating the process over and over again

This section of the book is where I will talk about the systems that you can put in place now to have a thriving business right now and all the way through as a Diamond. Believe me, if you start this now, you will save yourself a lot of worry and headaches later.

What is something unique about yourself? What makes you YOU?

What is a role that you do that anyone can do?

Income Producing Activities

Income Producing Activities, or IPAs, are the things that you should actively be doing to grow your business. For something to be an IPA, you should be able to track the effectiveness on your current month's paycheck.

Yes, you CAN have a thriving YL business just by accomplishing these tasks. And you can work 40 hours a week and have 0 members on your team. It's all based on if the type of work that you are doing is bringing in income.

To simplify IPAs, I have grouped them into the three E's:

EDUCATE:

How you are teaching, sharing, and exposing others to your products

ENROLL:

Having prospectives join as members, and members finding health with Essential Rewards

EMPOWER:

Encouraging members via follow-through, supporting their usage questions, engaging & coaching business members

The Hub

This is the foundation of it all. It is your oil usage and how comfortable you are with the product. And along with that is your personal development. This is so important because it will lay the foundation for how successful you are with your IPA tasks.

Please hear me out on this. You need personal development. You should have a love of these products and a basic understanding. You do NOT need to master either of these before you get started sharing and building a business.

If I had waited until I knew it all, you wouldn't be sitting here today.
— D. Gary Young

So what can actually be considered an IPA? Here are some ideas, though this is not an exhaustive list:

Educate

- Share a tidbit with a member/prospective
- Teach about the monthly promo products
- Attend and edify events led by other educators
- Be present and active in business and member groups
- Use products in public
- Share on social media (1 oil post: 5 personal posts)
- Add value to others' lives with a story
- Carry samples and exchange information

Enroll

- Enroll at least 2 new members every month (for growth)
- Teach 1 product-centered workshop each month
- Edify and market 1 product-centered workshop from an upline for your organization to attend
- Post an ER unboxing video
- Checking the VO for order completions and order errors
- Enroll new or existing members in Essential Rewards

Empower

- Respond to all communication
- Following 5 new people daily, commenting and engaging in content
- Commenting on 5 existing member or prospective member threads daily
- Checking with 0 PV members
- Sending private messages, texts, calls
- Send rank congratulation gifts or cards
- Talk to educators and leaders about their goals and how you can help them

Organizing Your IPAs

It's one thing to commit to doing IPAs. It's another thing to organize yourself. There are many different ways to have an effective system in place. Some are planner people. Some love notebooks. Some are all digital. Below are some of my favorite tools:

Virtual Office:

You can access each member's account information & simple stats via My Organization > their name. Use the Notes tab to write information, such as their preferred contact method, personal details, and incentives sent. Get into the habit of jotting notes down immediately after each conversation.

To Do Lists:

This is where I put all of my to-do lists and IPA activities. Certain apps will sync with your phone and computer, and you can even invite other users to access your lists and assign tasks to them. Plus, you can assign due dates, reminder notifications, and repeated events. So this can easily be your Everything Accountability tool.

Follow-Through Tasks

There are certain things that you can do on a regular basis to stay connected with your members and to make sure that you don't wait until the end of the month to wrap up the loose ends. Trust me, the last thing you want is to wait to flip ranks or get any issues settled on the last day of the month.

These are the tasks that you should plan on doing daily, weekly, and monthly. I call them "follow-through" tasks because they are cyclical. When you "follow up," there is an ending to the task, but these are items that you do regularly to help you build continuity, momentum, and growth.

Your JPA Schedule

This is a sample timeline of what you can do daily, weekly, biweekly, and monthly to keep your business growing.

Every Day:

- Check VO for upcoming orders that are close to a promo level
- Check VO for unprocessed orders and message them
- Connect with prospects

Every Week:

- Check in with any new members (within the last month)

Every 2 Weeks:

- Contact 0 PV members (9th and 26th)

Every Month:

- Newsletter out (4th)
- Rank up card/mailing (7th)
- Reach out to members from 3 months ago (10th)
- Missing ER dates (13th)
- Reach out to members from 2 months ago (16th)
- Reach out to last month's new members (19th)
- Reach Out to "Last Order Date Greater Than 3 Months" Accounts (24th)

For an expanded list and how-to scripts, consult with *Propel*.

Put these dates on your calendar. If you have an electronic calendar or to do list, set monthly reminders. Even if you don't have the members on your team yet, set them up now.

New Member & Prospective Check Ins

It's important that, from the beginning, you have a way to check in with your prospectives and new members. The first three months of a new membership are the most critical for continuation. If they are enthusiastic, enjoy the products they purchase, and find a need for other lifestyle changes based on our catalog, they will probably be a member for life. So because of this, at the end of each meeting, set up your next time to talk.

> **Business Builder Suggestion: As soon as you sign up a new member, mark on the calendar or your to-do list app when you will do your follow-ups with that person. That way they are set and you won't forget.**

The idea with this is that you should stay on top of who you talk to. It is easy to fall behind and lose your system. If that happens to you, don't feel discouraged. Just do better next time!

So how do I do this?

When I speak to someone (member or prospective), I get an idea from that conversation of how soon I should follow up again with them. Instead of checking that person off the list, I simply change the due date, so I will get a reminder when it's time to contact them again.

You will find that some people can eventually be taken off your "check in list" because they become such good friends that you talk often.

Who goes on the Member Check In list?

Anyone who I personally enrolled.

Who goes on the Prospective Check In list?

Anyone that I've talked to about oils or who I plan to talk to about oils.

How often should I check in with new members?

I recommend checking in with new members once a week for the first month of that member's time with Young Living (4 weeks), then once a month for Months 2 and 3.

UPON SIGNING UP

Create a plan with the new member to use at least 3 products from the kit in easy-to-do ways. You can use the Health Goals Worksheet from page 19 for this as well.

Week 1

Check in with the new member:

- "How are you feeling?"
- "What are you loving?"
- "What are you finding that you're nervous to try?"

Give simple ideas for using 3 oils.

Week 2

- "What are you loving/nervous to use?"
- "What supplies would make your oil use easier?"

Give simple ideas for using 3 more oils.

Week 3

- "How are you feeling? Do you notice a difference?"
- "Let's talk about some targeted support"

Give ideas for 3 complementary products to use alongside the oils they have.

Week 4

- "What has been your experience in our group and at our local events?"
- "Which is the product that you find yourself using the most?"
- "Which products are running low?"

Discuss the need for Essential Rewards to continue their original health goals and reordering products.

Professionalism & Conscious Language

Simply put, conscious language is what got us to become a strong and formidable team. It is what has built this community. It is the positive and warm-and-fuzzy feeling you get when you hear me talk about these oils.

Conscious Language is using your vocabulary precisely. Instead of picking my brain... ouch! Let's call it what it is. Let's have a mind-expanding conversation.

Instead of "I really want to become a Silver." No. Stop. Delete. "I am a Silver with a team of strong leaders and motivated members."

It's not that you are speaking lies. You are putting out into the world what you desire to come back. Words have meaning. Own the meaning of them. Be intentional, and know that your brain is listening to what you say.

I'll tell you my example of Conscious Language before I even knew what it was. I was a new builder and starting to grow our local community. I hosted monthly dinners but only 2-3 people would show up. But I would enthusiastically talk about our amazing community of oilers. We share ideas, laugh, talk about oil usage, and we have wonderful dinners! Did I lie? Nope! Not at all. Because for those that came, that's exactly what we did.

Within months, well, it happened. We now have dinners with many times the numbers from the beginning, and we are growing. I put out in the world what I envisioned, and look where it led. Did it hurt me to say it? No. The growth is there in the numbers.

I'll tell you something else that happened: I've experienced great success in enrollments. You want to know how I did it? Before vendor shows or workshop, I will say with spirit "I am attracting confident, excited, and determined women to me by sharing Young Living." And boy, did I! Several were members of other companies. Some were members of competitors. And some were strangers. I said that I would bring them in, and I did.

So as you are starting with Conscious Language, just take one word and delete it from your vocabulary. Maybe start with "Want." Want means a lack in something, so you are always trying to come from behind. Is that really how you want to go through life? No. So maybe instead of "I want..." say "I am attaining..." or "I am achieving..." Do it for one week and see how it feels.

Do you desire to change one more thing from your vocabulary? "Try" and "maybe." Right now, I want you to try to stand up. Did you? The answer is either yes or no. So you didn't "try" at all. You stood up or your didn't. Make a choice and stick by it. Try is just another word for "no." You will be amazed at what that little change will do for your life.

Create an affirmation, write it out, and tape it to your bathroom mirror. Say it to yourself every day, morning and night.

EXTRA CREDIT:
Pair an uplifting and motivating oil to smell while you say the affirmation out loud.

EXTRA EXTRA CREDIT:
Stand in a power pose while smelling your oil and saying your affirmation.

Understanding Educational Opportunities

Look, I know that there are some wonderful resources out there for you to further your Young Living Business. I encourage each person to look and find what works best for you and your specific learning styles.

Take the time to implement the teachings in this book. Follow through with the action steps. Allow yourself that time to have a strong foundation for your business.

I highly recommend, as a next step, to invest in *Propel* as a platform to grow and maintain the business that you have started here with this book. These two books are meant to be companion pieces, building on the lessons, ideas, and depth of understanding in the YL business. *Propel* is the book that provides you with the tools to take ownership of your business. So reach out to your upline, enroller, and crossline friends and start an accountability team to take this business further.

Beyond that, make sure that you understand the Virtual Office. This is crucial to your success as a leader. There is a wealth of knowledge right at our fingertips, and the more that you understand what is there, you can suggest to your members to do the same.

When you have others on your team that express interest in learning more about the Young Living business, give them their own copy of this book. This book is for everyone, whether someone is just getting started and wants to have the right systems in place or if someone got to Executive or Silver and now needs help getting back to the basics. Write them a little note of encouragement with your Why. That will make a big difference. They already have connected with you when they became a member on your team. Now, give them this glimpse into your motivation for the business.

Finally, I encourage you to be ok with your members learning from others. They may really connect with you and find that they can learn great lessons from and with you. Or they may connect better with another leader. Whichever their path, they are still on your team. And really, so what if they find a mentor in someone else? It's ok that you're not everything to everyone. Your role is a guide so that they can find their own path.

Just remember that the same things that you do when you first start are the same things that you do at Diamond and above. It's just a rinse and repeat model.

Welcome to your Young Living business. This is very exciting because you have all of your goals and possibilities ahead of you. But now it's on you. I can teach you how to climb a mountain, but I cannot place you on top of it. You have to do the work. You will work harder and grow more than you ever thought possible. I am excited for you in taking your next step to the possibilities. You just have to do it.

Getting Paid

To put it simply, you make money with Young Living when you enroll someone with a PSK or when they make additional purchases. If they sign up a new member, you make a smaller commission from that purchase too.

While you are a Distributor, Star, Senior Star, and Executive, you can get paid 4 different ways:

Commission Type	What You Earn	Requirements for Earning
Start Living Bonus	Earn a 1 time $25 cash bonus	**You:** Spend 50 PV **They:** Purchase a Premium Starter Kit
Fast Start Bonus	Earn a 25% bonus on new, personally enrolled distributor's orders	**You:** Spend 50 PV **They:** Purchase anything with PV in the first 3 calendar months of their membership
Rising Star Bonus	1, 3, 6 shares (approximately $50 each share) for having 3, 5, and 7 active legs in your organization (building to Silver, Platinum, and RCD)	**You:** Spend 100 PV **They:** spend 100 PV on ER (top of the leg), and 300, 500, or 1000 OGV
Unilevel Commissions	Earn a commission between 4-8% of the PV of the purchases by members on various levels in your organization	**You:** Spend 100 PV **They:** Purchase anything with PV at any point in their membership

How much do you need to spend each month? If you want to earn the $50 bonus from sign-ups with the PSK, you simply need to spend 50 PV in a month. To earn full commission on other purchases, you need to spend 100 PV in that month.

Need a full explanation of the compensation plan? Online tutorials and videos are your friends!

I want to stress that it is important for you to take ownership of understanding the compensation plan on your own. There are different learning styles and needs, and that is why I am not explicitly explaining the full comp plan here in this book. I promise, once you study it enough to make sense, then it will be much more satisfying.

Feeling overwhelmed? Just focus on where you are now + 2 ranks higher. And I want to empower you in this: you can start sharing before you know the compensation plan inside and out. The basics that I teach in this book will get you started with the right structures you need, and you can learn the rest as you go.

Do a web search for "simple explanation" of our compensation plan. Enjoy!

Setting Up For Success: Strategic Placement

Because you are starting this business off with gusto and having success at signing up new members (conscious language talking here), we feel the need to make sure you understand some basics on how to lay out your team. You can get an even more in-depth explanation in *Propel*.

There are two schools of thought:

1. Find your goal paycheck using the Young Living Income Disclosure Statement. Now take however many legs you need to get there and add one. That's going to be what you will work to build and restructure.

2. Aim for the top and set yourself up for 7 legs (6 needed for Royal Crown Diamond + one extra for PGV).

So how do you actually get those legs moving along? Strategic Placement! This is where you continue as the enroller and make the new member's sponsor be someone in a different downline.

How do you choose where they go?

First, look at geography. You can build your legs based on where people live. After all, local communities can make this business stronger!

Next, consider family relationships or friendships. If someone knows another person who is already a member, then that's a natural sponsor option.

Finally, look at who is actively using essential oils and/or might be a potential business builder in the future. Having a downline that you help build could be the motivation that they need to move forward in the business in a big way. If the personalities might match up, then that could be a great partnership.

Regardless, when I strategically place someone, I always have a conversation with the new sponsor to make sure that they are committed to staying on ER with a minimum purchase of 100 PV (so they can earn commission). I also always set up a 3-way conversation with the new member, sponsor, and myself so that everyone can be on the same page and get to know each other. My end goal is to build a relationship between the sponsor and member so that I can be there, but I am not necessary for the successful experience for that new member.

How do you explain it to people?

To the sponsor: "I love how enthusiastic you are in using/sharing Young Living. Thank you for your loyalty! I would love to be able to help you earn a little bit back to help you pay for your oil purchases. Would you be willing to let me help you with that by connecting you with future members? I have one in mind for you, and I think you would get along great!"

To the new member: "I want to introduce you to _____. She is a wonderful resource and friend! Like you, she _____. The best thing about this is that you have two of us immediately that can answer questions, you can lean on for advice, and who are here to support you in your membership and health."

There is no magic ball.

Just because you do all the right steps doesn't mean that you are going to have the perfect number of legs that all continue on ER indefinitely and decide to grow their business because of your help. It may happen, but it may not. And you may end up lopsided. There is no correct answer, as a lot of it will come from your instinct. This is a time when, if you are looking at places for new members, talk to your upline who can help you strategize.

Remember, the best option is to group people together based on what you have learned from FORMing and building the relationship and knowing what you already know about your business builders and placing them there. It's intuition, reading people, and relationship-building.

The Wellness Line

- Normal body functions and systems
- YL oils and products support these normal body functions and systems
- No claims made
- No ailments made

WELLNESS LINE

- Abnormal body functions and systems
- Saying that YL oils and products can take your health from below the line to above it
- Making disease claims
- Listing specific ailments

Young Living has created some wonderful information regarding what you can and can't say when sharing these products and this lifestyle. This is all available in your Virtual Office, but I still want to discuss it here.

Let's look at a typical, healthy person. They are at or above the Wellness Line. That means each of the products are able to support their already-healthy body.

As a Young Living Distributor (and even as a member), you have agreed that you are not diagnosing, curing, or preventing any disease or sick state of being. That is below the Wellness Line. According to Congress and US government agencies, only pharmaceuticals can treat, cure, or prevent illness or disease. Essential oils are classified as either beauty products or dietary supplements so they do not fit in the category of pharmaceuticals.

Why are we so happy for this classification as a beauty or dietary supplement? Because it means that we can purchase what we want, when we want it. If these were classified as pharmaceuticals, we could only get them through doctors or pharmacists, with a prescription.

So you know what we can't say, now what can you say?

- How these oils and supplements make you feel (energy, sleep, emotions, physical sensations can all be appropriate).

- How oils can support living a life with wellness, purpose, and abundance.

- How Young Living oils from the Vitality Line are safe to consume as a dietary supplement.

- How supplements can support our immune system, muscles, ligaments, tendons, and other body systems.

- How oils can support and maintain body systems, age-related conditions, natural body functions, and occasional emotional states.

- How Young Living's Seed to Seal promise positively influences the products, members, and quality.

A couple of notes:

- When in doubt, look at the Young Living-published descriptions.

- When speaking of supporting an internal body system, you are only talking about Vitality oils and supplements.

Remember, if you avoid these, you'll be fine:

- Don't instruct anyone to use an oil as a medical drug.

- Don't make medical testimonials to promote products.

- Don't prescribe, diagnose, or treat functions or dysfunctions of the mind or body for humans or animals.

- Don't instruct a sick person on how to become well.

Create a testimonial. Pick an oil. How does this support your already-healthy body?

A Do & Don't Guide From Other Leaders

I interviewed some of the top Silver+ leaders in the company, and these are some of their suggestions in starting your YL Business:

DON'T	DO
Announce on social media that you sell oils and message if interested	Share a story of product usage and the importance in your life
Try to know it all or wait to share until you're an expert	Know how to say "I don't know," and "Let's go find that answer together."
Cut and paste from other sources	Use your own voice and personality
Give in to Analysis Paralysis	Jump in and know that you will learn as you go. Nothing changes in your comfort zone.
Think you know everything about this business	Understand that the business changes and it's good to change with it
Start a separate business profile for each of your social media outlets	Tap into the resources provided by your upline. Don't have an active direct upline? Contact YL Customer Service to get the names of your Silver, Gold, Platinum, and Diamond leaders and reach out to them for guidance.
Think that people will always come to you.	Start a follow up system early. This will get you in a good habit so that you can grow your business exponentially. Follow ups are not about selling, but they are about connecting with people. Increased sales will follow.
Just put all of your new members in your Level 1.	Work with your upline to strategize and utilize strategic placements
Get distracted by multiple avenues. Stick to one business.	See the big picture and how much potential exists in this business, without the extra side hustles.
Get caught up in the short-term benefits of friends adding on to your orders	Encourage empowerment by allowing them to purchase their own membership and PSK (or at the bare minimum, as Basic Kit)
Compare yourself and your business to others	Understand that you are unique and your situation is your own. Take the ups and downs and allow it to inspire you to further greatness.

Notes

Gary and Mary Young chose a **multi-level marketing structure** for Young Living so they could focus on product development and running the business. This allows those using the products (Distributors) to market, educate, and recruit as desired.

WHAT IS THE DIFFERENCE?

Network Marketing

Using your network of friends and their friends to make connections and build relationships

Direct Sales

Have an event to sell products and earn commissions with additional commission for each team member

Multi-Level Marketing

A type of Network Marketing with a spider-plant pattern to reach new cold-to-warm markets

Pyramid Scheme

An illegal investment where original investors directly take money from new enrollees and buy-ins

WHERE DOES THE MONEY GO?

Traditional Retail

- 30-40% to Corporate
  50-60% to Warehouse

- 20% Kept at local store

MLM

- 50% to Corporate for sales, packaging, warehouse, customer service, events

- **50% Given to Independent Distributors**

BENEFITS OF A NETWORK MARKETING STRUCTURE

You are your own boss

Don't have to keep stock or manage distribution

Residual income and unending earning possibilities

Cutting the market middleman

YOUNG LIVING TERMS

Enroller:
The person responsible for introducing a new member to Young Living. Enrollers are eligible to qualify for financial bonuses, including the Fast Start and Starter Kit bonuses.

Sponsor:
A new member's direct upline and main support. The sponsor may also be the enroller.

PV (Personal Volume):
The total monthly volume of your personal orders.

OGV (Organization Group Volume):
The monthly volume of your entire organization.

PGV (Personal Group Volume):
The monthly volume in an organization, excluding any Silver or higher rank volume and any qualifying leg(s) volume.

Leg:
Each personally sponsored member is considered first level and a separate leg within an organization.

LV (Leg Volume) @ OGV:
The number of legs and the amount of monthly OGV required for each leg to qualify for each rank.

Level:
The position of a member within an organization. Members who are directly sponsored by another member are considered the sponsoring member's first level. Those members who are sponsored by a member's first level are considered that member's second level and so on.

Compression:
If a member does not meet the 100 PV qualification to earn commissions, his or her volume, if any, is combined, or "compressed", with all the volume of members down to and including the next qualifying member in the organization with at least 100 PV.

Unilevel:
A term used to define the percentage of commission earned for each level. Qualifying members with 100 PV earn 8% on the PV of each member on the first level within their organization, 5% on the second level, and 4% on the third through fifth levels depending on rank achieved that month.

Personal Generation Commissions:
Additional commissions are paid to members who achieve the rank of Silver or higher on all volume within each leg of the organization, down to but excluding the next Silver or higher ranked member within the leg.

Generation:
A Silver or higher ranked member and his or her entire organization.

Generation Commissions:
Based on a member's monthly rank of Silver or higher, an additional 3% commission is paid on the OGV of each Silver or higher in the member's organization. This commission is paid down to the next Silver or higher ranked member and down to eight generations deep in each leg.

Essential Rewards (ER):
Members are encouraged to sign up for this autoship program in which they order products that are automatically shipped to them each month. The member's ER order may be changed each month. Essential Rewards purchases earn the member ER points redeemable for free product. A minimum 50 PV is required, although 100 PV is required for the Rising Star Team Bonus.

MONTHLY BUSINESS GOALS

Fill out this form one month at a time in order to set your monthly goals.

	Mo ____	Mo ____	Mo ____	Mo ____	Mo ____	Mo ____
Team Size						
Total Members						
Members with PV						
OGV (Overall Group Volume)						
New Members This Month						
% of Super Recruiters						
% of Team Growth						
New Rankers						
Avg PV Per Ordering Member						
Member % ER						
Members on ER						
Enrollers						
Percent Enrollers						
My Enrollments						
My Paycheck						
My Rank						

MONTHLY BUSINESS TRACKER

All of these statistics come from the Oily Tools app, however if you wanted, you can figure them out yourself.
Use this as a way to reflect on the accomplishments of the month.

	Mo ___	Mo ___	Mo ___	Mo ___	Mo ___	Mo ___
Team Size						
Total Members						
Members with PV						
OGV (Overall Group Volume)						
New Members This Month						
% of Super Recruiters						
% of Team Growth						
New Rankers						
Avg PV Per Ordering Member						
Member % ER						
Members on ER						
Enrollers						
Percent Enrollers						
My Enrollments						
My Paycheck						
My Rank						

MONTHLY GOAL PLAN

Personal Enrollment Goal: _____   Total Team Member Goal: _____

Current Rank: _____   Rank Goal: _____

Current Members on ER: _____ x 1.2 =_____ (goal members on ER this month)

My Revolving List of Prospects

Posts to Facebook/Instagram/Social Media

☐ Personal: ☐ Personal: ☐ Personal:

☐ Personal: ☐ Personal: ☐ Personal:

☐ Personal: ☐ Personal: ☐ Personal:

☐ Oils: ☐ Oils: ☐ Oils:

☐ Do one Facebook Live

☐ Teach one Facebook Intro for yourself/prospects
  Date of class: Host:
  # Invited: .   # Actively Attended:

☐ Teach one Facebook Intro for members on your team *(focus on creating legs)*
  Date of class: Host:
  # Invited: # Actively Attended:

☐ Attend two in-person events *(focus on building this importance of local community)*

☐ Have six attendees to in-person events

☐ I will send samples and a handwritten note to these six people:

☐ I will read one personal growth/leadership book:

This is a place to start if you are launching or relaunching your business. Don't limit yourself to just this sheet. You may want to challenge yourself by adding onto these target goals.

WELLNESS WORKSHOP NOTES

My Interests & Health Goals:

General Wellness · Winter Wellness · Pregnancy
Childbirth · Babies · Children · Mood & Emotions
Stress · Clear Thinking · Immune System
Digestive System · Respiratory Support · Healthy Skin
Oral Hygiene · Skeletal System · Weight Management
Beauty & Skin Care · Makeup · Toxin-Free Cleaning
Sleep · Athletics · Pet & Animal · Making Money

Products Discussed

1.

2.

3.

4.

5.

6.

7.

8.

9.

10.

11.

12.

My Plan

1.

2.

3.

**Keep These
People in Mind**

Host Information

Name:_____

YL#: _____

Contact Info: _____

_____

Resources:
- YoungLiving.com
- discoverLSP.com
- inspiredsharing.com

MY UPLINE & CROSSLINE CONTACTS

GROUPS   WEBSITES

MY SIGN UP LINK:

My Daily Affirmations

Notes

Notes